TOP 10 WOMEN TENNIS PLAYERS

Denis J. Harrington

SPORTS TOP 10

Enslow Publishers, Inc.

40 Industrial Road	PO Box 38
Box 398	Aldershot
Berkeley Heights, NJ 07922	Hants GU12 6BP
USA	UK

http://www.enslow.com

Library of Congress Cataloging-in-Publication Data

Harrington, Denis J., 1932–
    Top 10 Women Tennis Players / Denis J. Harrington.
        p. cm.—(Sports Top 10)
    Includes index.
    ISBN 0-89490-612-7
    1. Women tennis players—Biography—Juvenile literature.
[1. Tennis players. 2. Women—Biography.] I. Title. II. Title:
Top ten women tennis players. III. Series.
GV994.A1H36 1995
796.342'092'2—dc20
[B]   94-31888
                                       CIP
                                       AC
Printed in the United States of America

10 9 8 7 6 5 4 3

Photo Credits: International Tennis Hall of Fame, pp. 6, 9, 11, 13, 23, 25; © Russ Adams
Productions, Inc., pp. 14, 17, 18, 21, 26, 29, 31, 33, 35, 37, 39, 41, 42, 45.

Cover Photo: © Russ Adams Productions, Inc.

Interior Design: Richard Stalzer

CONTENTS

INTRODUCTION

THE GAME OF TENNIS is more than one-hundred years old. In this time there have been many great women champions. The players I have chosen are important for reasons other than just their skill and ability.

Althea Gibson was the first African-American woman to reach the top in tennis. She broke the "color line" in major tournaments both in the United States and overseas. Despite growing up poor, she found a way to become the best of the best. Her story gave hope to millions of people around the world.

What's more, she changed the way women played tennis. She learned to serve the ball hard. Then she would rush the net for overhead smashes and winning volleys. Before Gibson, serve-and-volley tennis was thought to be a style only for men.

Maureen Connolly claimed all the important championships while she was still a teenager. She helped stir the interest of young people everywhere.

No one has more Grand Slam titles than Margaret Court. From 1960 through 1975 the powerful Australian won twenty-four singles crowns. She also won nineteen titles each in doubles and mixed doubles. The total number of Grand Slam titles Court won in these years was an amazing sixty-two! She has been called the greatest woman tennis player of all time.

Billie Jean King fought for women's rights in professional tennis—equal pay and treatment. She also began a new pro tour. Yet she still found time to be one of the game's great champions.

Chris Evert made the two-fisted backhand popular. She stayed at the top of the world rankings longer than anyone before her.

During the 1980s Martina Navratilova all but rewrote the record books. She also introduced women tennis players to working out with weights and other new training methods.

Steffi Graf, Zina Garrison-Jackson, Monica Seles, and Gabriela Sabatini (who retired in 1996) have brought new talent and excitement to the game. Because of their shotmaking abilities and colorful personalities, more people are filling tennis stadiums in every country around the globe. As a result women's tennis has never been more prosperous.

For these reasons the women profiled in this book are my choice for "Top 10 Women Tennis Players." After reading about their accomplishments you may agree or you may have your own choices.

SINGLES CHAMPIONSHIP WINS

Player	Australian	French	Wimbledon	U.S.
MAUREEN CONNOLLY	'53	'53, '54	'52, '53, '54	'51, '52, '53
MARGARET COURT	'60–'66, '69, '70, '71, '73	'62, '64, '69, '70, '73	'63, '65, '70	'62, '65, '69, '70, '73
CHRIS EVERT	'82, '84	'74, '75, '79, '80, '83, '85, '86	'74, '76, '81	'75, '76, '77, '78, '80, '82
ZINA GARRISON-JACKSON			F: '90	S: '88, '89
ALTHEA GIBSON		'56	'57, '58	'57, '58
STEFFI GRAF	'88, '89, '90, '94	'87, '88, '93, '95, '96	'88, '89, '91, '92, '93, '95, '96	'88, '89, '93, '95, '96
BILLIE JEAN KING	'68	'72	'66, '67, '68, '72, '73, '75	'67, '71, '72, '74
MARTINA NAVRATILOVA	'81, '83, '85	'82, '84	'78, '79, '82, '83, '84, '85, '86, '87, '90	'83, '84, '86, '87
GABRIEL SABATINI			F: '91	'90, S: '95
MONICA SELES	'91, '92, '93, '96, S: '99	'90, '91, '92, S: '97, F: '98, SF: '99	F: '92	'91, '92, F: '95, '96

F: Finalist   S: Semi-Finalist

MAUREEN CONNOLLY

Maureen Connolly was short and slight of build with the look of the girl next door. But on the court she was a tiger— one of the most fierce competitors ever to play tennis.

MAUREEN CONNOLLY

TENNIS HISTORY WAS IN THE making. The spectators at the West Side Tennis Club in New York could sense it. So could Shirley Fry.

Across the net from Fry, Maureen Connolly leaped to return a lob. The ball streaked off her racquet to a far corner of the court. There it kicked up a spray of lime dust. "Point!" the referee announced, acknowledging that Connolly's ball landed in the court.

Shirley Fry had fought the good fight. After losing the first set she rallied to win the second. But the third and deciding set was steadily slipping away from her.

Fry was very tired. She saw the ball barely clear the tape. It dipped and bounced softly off the forecourt grass. Shirley ran on weary legs to make the shot.[1] Her effort was too strong.

"Out! Point and match, Miss Connolly."

Cheering shook the Forest Hills stadium. At sixteen, Maureen Connolly became the youngest player ever to win the U.S. Championship. The year was 1951.

Several months later Connolly played Louise Brough for the 1952 All-England title at Wimbledon, England. Their match was one of the most exciting in the tournament's long history.[2] But in the end, true grit and powerful ground strokes earned Connolly the victory. During the trophy presentation she said, "This is the happiest day of my life."[3]

In 1953, Maureen Connolly achieved a significant first for a woman. She put together a Grand Slam. Within the same year, she won the major championships of Australia, France, England, and the United States.

The next year Connolly repeated her French and Wimbledon

victories. Then she went home to rest. While horseback riding she seriously injured her right leg when a passing truck sideswiped her horse. Suddenly, at nineteen, Connolly's career was over.

With the speed of a shooting star she had climbed to the heights. And just as quickly she faded from the scene. Despite such a short stay at the top, Maureen Connolly managed to light up the tennis skies as few players have ever done.

A San Diego sports writer nicknamed Maureen "Little Mo."[4] He compared her cannon-like shots to the big guns of the battleship *U.S.S. Missouri*. At times it must have seemed that way to her opponents.

MAUREEN CONNOLLY

BORN: September 17, 1934, San Diego, California.

HEIGHT: 5 feet, 5 inches; WEIGHT: 127 pounds.

EDUCATION: Cathedral (San Diego) High School; No college.

HONORS: Member U.S. Wightman Cup Team: 1951-1954; Ranked No. 1 Woman Player in the World, 1952-1954; Associated Press Female Athlete of the Year, 1951-1953; International Tennis Hall of Fame, 1968; Helms Foundation Hall of Fame, 1968.

CAREER EARNINGS: Played all of her career as an amateur.

DIED: June 21, 1969 (of cancer).

Unlike many other women tennis champions, Maureen Connolly liked to play at the net. She had quick reflexes and the shotmaking ability to pass her opponents with winning returns down either sideline.

MARGARET COURT

MORE THAN TWO HOURS HAD passed in the wind-blown heat on Wimbledon's famous Centre Court. Margaret Court could barely run. She had torn ligaments in her left ankle. And the pain-killing medicine for her injury had worn off. Every move was now a matter of courage.[1]

Across the net from Margaret Court, Billie Jean King was hobbled by severe leg cramps. She could no longer come to the net to volley. Instead she had to stay on the baseline, hitting lobs and deep drives.

The first set lasted a record twenty-six games! Margaret Court won the set, 14–12. In the second set, leading 10–9, she stretched for a passing shot and fell heavily.[2] A groan went up from the spectators who had crowded into the stands. Margaret Court rose slowly to a soft ripple of applause.

On the next exchange Court managed to return a hard forehand smash. Billie Jean King chopped the ball down the far sideline. Gathering all her strength, Court banged a low drive crosscourt into the corner. In a desperate attempt to stave off defeat, Billie Jean King countered with a lunging forehand. But the ball failed to clear the net. The set finally ended, 11–9.

Court had won the women's 1970 All-England Championship. The title was her third major tournament victory of the year. Following the forty-six game ordeal, she told reporters, "I don't know if I could have played a third set. When I came off the court I had a cramp in the ankle quite badly."[3]

Tennis began for Margaret Court when she was still a young girl in Australia. A neighbor gave her an old racquet, and she promptly fell in love with the game. She and her

Margaret Court worked hard to perfect her game. But she particularly trained herself not to make the same mistake twice in a match. She believed that mental errors were more costly than the physical ones.

brothers played for hours on public courts near their home. "The boys banged balls at me as hard as they could," she said, "and I just had to reach them if we wanted to go on playing."[4]

Lean and tall with long arms, she seemed to have been born to play tennis. At age seventeen she became the youngest player ever to win an Australian National singles title. Just seven years later she retired from the competitive grind, saying, "I've won everything, and I'm bored with tennis."[5]

After marrying in 1967, she returned to the tournament scene. She experienced the high point of her career. It was in the women's final of the 1970 U.S. Open.

Court split the first two sets with Rosemary Casals. Then she put on dazzling displays of power and shotmaking ability. In the third set her lobs kicked up baseline chalk time and time again. She mixed lobs with overhead smashes and forehand drives that Casals simply couldn't return.

As the shadows grew long across the worn turf of Forest Hills (New York) stadium, Casals netted her last serve. Court had won a Grand Slam! She had won Wimbledon as well as the Australian, French and U.S. Opens—all in the same year. She became only the second woman ever to achieve this feat.

Margaret Court retired for good in 1977. At that time her longtime mixed doubles partner Marty Riessen, said, "She should go down as the finest woman player ever."[6]

MARGARET COURT

BORN: July 16, 1942, Albury, New South Wales, Australia.

HEIGHT: 5 feet, 9 inches; WEIGHT: 140 pounds.

EDUCATION: Local elementary, secondary schools. No college.

HONORS: Seventeen Virginia Slims Tournaments; seventy-nine singles titles; sixty-two Grand Slam titles (singles, doubles, and mixed doubles); seventy-five matches (twenty-five in succession): 1973; Ranked No. 1 Woman Player in the World: 1962-1965, 1970, 1971, 1973, 1974; International Tennis Hall of Fame, 1979.

CAREER EARNINGS: $550,000 (played most of her career as an amateur).

Margaret Court had no tennis weaknesses—nothing that would give any edge to an opponent. She used her height and long reach to hit powerful shots from either the forehand or backhand sides.

CHRIS EVERT

Concentration was always the strongest part of Chris Evert's game. From her earliest days as a player, she put special emphasis on mastering technique. This single-mindedness stayed with her through the years.

CHRIS EVERT

ON JULY 5, 1974, CHRIS Evert played in the women's finals of the All England Championships for the first time. Most of the spectators at Wimbledon that day came to cheer for the pixie-like nineteen-year-old.[1] They did so loudly when she won the opening set, 6–0, against Olga Morozova of the Soviet Union. But they grew quiet when the Russian woman rallied strongly in the second set to trail only 4–3.

A serve came in flat and hard. Evert banged a crossing backhand drive. Morozova managed to return Evert's shot with topspin. The ball bounded high, and Evert barely got her racquet on it. With an overhead smash, Olga put away the soft lob for a winner.

During the next exchange, Evert hit a forehand deep to the corner. Morozova reached the ball and countered with a drop shot. Evert lunged and sent a weak chop into the forecourt. Morozova charged the net and blasted a passing shot for a winner. The set was now even at 4–4.

Evert calmly returned to the baseline and kept swinging.[2] She won the next game with a forehand that caught Morozova out of position. Once again her shots were crisp and controlled. The contest ended suddenly when Morozova double faulted on her serve. The Russian lost the set, 6–4, as well as the match.

A year later Christ Evert faced Evonne Goolagong Cawley of Australia for the U.S. Open title. Cawley took an early lead, displaying a strong attack at the net.[3] The Australian hung on to win the first set, 7–5.

Evert rallied with steady two-handed returns. Her shots forced Cawley to make costly errors. Evert finished strongly to claim the second set, 6–4, and tie the match.

In the third set Cawley began rushing the net again. This time, Evert won the crucial points with well-placed shots along the sidelines. Evert swept through the last four games to win the championship.

With these victories Chris Evert began her twelve-year reign as the "Queen of Tennis."[4] During this period she was ranked the No. 1 woman player in the world five times. She also became the first competitor—male or female—to win 1,000 matches. And on clay courts she proved to be nearly unbeatable. Because of her intense concentration and unflappable disposition, the British press dubbed Chris Evert the "Ice Dolly."[5]

From her earliest days in tennis Evert wanted to win. She once used the words "ruthless" and "determined" to describe her approach to the game. Patience was another of her outstanding qualities as a competitor. She could stay on the baseline and return everything her opponent hit.

This tactic bothered many of the leading players. Most of them simply weren't willing to just hit with her for long exchanges under a hot sun. After awhile they would try to force winning shots. But her steady, deep returns usually caught them off balance and out of position. She used their mistakes to beat them. It was her trademark.

Evert always kept in top condition. She trained hard. Her style of play called for superior stamina and endurance. In every match she set out to wear down her opponent. This meant she had to have a strong inner drive. And she did. Her mental toughness was the envy of the tennis world. No one in the history of the sport has managed to remain so focused, so dedicated, for so many years.

In 1986 she added a record seventh French Open title to her collection.[6] Three years later, at age thirty-four, she retired from tournament play. Chris Evert's accomplishments would forever be part of tennis history.

CHRIS EVERT

BORN: December 21, 1954, Fort Lauderdale, Florida.

HEIGHT: 5 feet, 6 inches; WEIGHT: 125 pounds.

EDUCATION: Local elementary, high schools. No college.

HONORS: U.S. Olympic Team, 1988; One or more major (Grand Slam) championships for 13 successive years; 157 singles titles; 1,309 singles matches; Ranked No. 1 Woman Player in the World, 1975-1977, 1980, 1981, 1985.

CAREER EARNINGS: $8,896,195.

With a two-fisted backhand, Chris Evert got more power and accuracy. But this method shortened her reach for some returns. So, she trained herself to run farther and longer than the other players.

ZINA GARRISON-JACKSON

Zina Garrison-Jackson is a precision shotmaker from anywhere on the court. She has one of the most complete games in all of women's tennis. For this reason, she is always hard to beat.

ZINA GARRISON-JACKSON

THE EXPERIENCE WAS BITTERSWEET FOR Zina Garrison-Jackson. Within a matter of moments she would win the biggest match of her life. But it also meant ending the career of the woman known for so long as the "Queen of Tennis," Chris Evert.[1]

Zina Garrison-Jackson had taken the first set, 7–6. She led by doing what she did best—returning shots from all over the court. Now, at match point in the second set, Garrison-Jackson was in control. Her serve went deep and hard to the baseline.

Evert hit a forehand crosscourt. Garrison-Jackson fielded the ball on the run, chopping it just over the net. With a supreme effort Evert managed a drop shot that softly kicked off the hard court surface. Garrison-Jackson wacked at the waist-high ball. Evert stretched to make the save, but missed.

The match was over, 6–2. Garrison-Jackson had beaten one of the greatest competitors ever to swing a racquet. Now she would advance to the semifinals of the 1989 U.S. Open. She rushed to the net, tears streaming down her face. She hugged Chris Evert, and they left they court in each other's arms.

"I wanted to win the match very badly," Garrison-Jackson said afterward, "but I had so much respect for Chris that I felt badly. That's what's so weird about that picture of us walking off the court. She's smiling and I'm crying."[2]

As for the strategy that won the historic victory, she said, "I just decided that everything Chris was going to hit, I was going to somehow get it back."[3]

That year Garrison-Jackson was ranked the No. 4 Woman Player in the World. Her ground strokes were a match for those of the best players in the game. And she covered the court with a catlike grace. But she still lacked one major weapon—a big serve.

In 1990, Garrison-Jackson made it to the finals of the All England Championships. That day she become only the second African-American woman ever to play on Centre Court. Watching the match was the first African-American woman to play there, Althea Gibson. Gibson won at Wimbledon in 1957 and 1958.

Garrison-Jackson lost the opening set, 6–4, after more than holding her own against Martina Navratilova. But in the second set, Navratilova's experience and power began to take their toll. Garrison-Jackson never gave up. She chased down and often returned Navratilova's best shots. Her lobs to the baseline were especially effective. Time and again they drove Navratilova back from the net.

Finally, at match point, Garrison-Jackson hit the ball long. She lost the second set, 6–1. Afterward, when the players shook hands, Navratilova whispered, "You'll probably win here one day."[4]

One of Garrison-Jackson's proudest moments came in 1988 when she won an Olympic Gold Medal in women's doubles. Her partner on the U.S. team was Pam Shriver.

Today Zina Garrison-Jackson has a much stronger serve. And in 1993 she won her thirteenth professional tournament. It's expected she will soon add a Grand Slam title to her growing collection.

Althea Gibson once said, "Champions need fast feet and at least one great shot. Zina has the feet but, as yet, not that one powerful shot."[5] Perhaps she'll find the one powerful shot that can win her a Grand Slam title.

ZINA GARRISON-JACKSON

BORN: November 16, 1963, Houston, Texas.

HEIGHT: 5 feet, 4-1/2 inches; WEIGHT: 135 pounds.

EDUCATION: Local public elementary, high schools. No college.

HONORS: Thirteen singles titles; Member U.S. Federation Cup Team:
1984–1987, 1989–1991; U.S. Wightman Cup Team: 1987, 1988.

CAREER EARNINGS: $4,013,373.

Of all of the tournaments, Zina Garrison-Jackson would like most to win at Wimbledon. "The first time I saw the championship trophy," she said, "I couldn't take my eyes off of it."

ALTHEA GIBSON

DESPITE ONE-HUNDRED-DEGREE HEAT and wilting pressure, Althea Gibson seemed cool and poised. She moved easily along the baseline—a tall, lean, muscled African-American woman. She was the first African American to ever play at the famed Wimbledon club in England. A capacity crowd that included Queen Elizabeth II watched. Such was the setting for the women's final of the 1957 All England Championships.

The strings of Gibson's racquet slammed against the ball with a hollow thudding sound. Little more than a blur, the ball streaked across the net, kicking low off the sun-bleached grass. Ace! Darlene Hard could merely salute another perfectly placed serve with a wave of her hand.[1]

Gibson had easily won the first set, 6–3. Now she was only one match point away from a tennis first. Once again she sent the ball rocketing into a far corner. Darlene Hard managed to lob it back. Then Gibson hit a powerful forehand return. Hard lunged, but missed the ball.

Racquet raised, Gibson shouted about her victory, "At last! At last!"[2] Old for tennis at age twenty-nine, she had finally completed her long climb to the top. Back home in New York, she was treated to a ticker tape parade down Broadway. Then it was on to the U.S. National Championships at Forest Hills.

In New York, Althea Gibson met Louise Brough in the finals. She trailed 2–3 early on, but rallied to take the opening set, 6–3. Brough fought back bravely. But Gibson's powerful ground strokes made the difference. Gibson hung on to win the second set, 6–2, and the women's title. The following year Gibson would once again capture the hearts and minds of the

ALTHEA GIBSON

Althea Gibson was a natural athlete. She could play to perfection any game requiring hand and eye coordination. Tennis was just such a game. Her records show that she truly played it to perfection.

tennis world. She defended her championships in both England and the United States.[3]

The place of her victory, the West Side Tennis Club in Forest Hills, New York, was only a matter of minutes from the Harlem neighborhood in which she first picked up a racquet, a paddle tennis racquet. Her family's apartment on 143rd Street was just a short walk from the Police Athletic League (PAL) paddle tennis courts. One summer morning she decided to try her hand at this new game. Before long, she was the champion on her block.

PAL supervisor Buddy Walker could see that Gibson had unusual athletic ability. He knew that she was already an outstanding softball and basketball player. He decided she should try real tennis. He bought her a used racquet and she began hitting balls against a wall in a local schoolyard. Later, he took her to play on some public courts in the area. That fall, at age fourteen, she began taking lessons at the Cosmopolitan Tennis Club in Harlem.

While still a teenager, she lived part of the year in Wilmington, North Carolina with the family of an African-American tennis official, Dr. Hubert Eaton. During the summer she stayed in Lynchburg, Virginia with the family of another African-American official, Dr. Robert Johnson. They sponsored her in American Tennis Association tournaments.

Looking back on those days, she said, "I really wasn't the tennis type. But I learned you could be a lady and still play like a tiger, and beat the liver and lights out of the ball."[4]

Not until 1950 did she finally receive an invitation to play in the U.S. Nationals. She lost her second-round match, but broke forever the "color line" in major tennis tournaments.

Although her stay in the spotlight was brief, Althea Gibson changed women's tennis in a way no one else ever did.

It was once written, "She served remarkably like a man, and played the whole game with strength and power."[5]

BORN: August 25, 1927, Silver, South Carolina.

HEIGHT: 5 feet, 11 inches; WEIGHT: 140 pounds.

EDUCATION: Wilmington (North Carolina) Industrial High School, Florida A & M University (B.S. degree in physical education).

HONORS: Ranked No. 1 Woman Player in the World: 1957, 1958; International Tennis Hall of Fame, 1971; International Women's Sports Hall of Fame: 1980.

CAREER EARNINGS: Played all of her career as an amateur.

Because of her power and range of motion, Althea Gibson played particularly well on fast grass courts. Both Wimbledon and Forest Hills had such a surface. These stadiums were the scenes of her greatest triumphs.

STEFFI GRAF

Steffi Graf had to work hard on her backhand. Once it was the weakest part of her game. But hours of hitting balls and playing against men helped her to solve this problem.

THE JETLINER SWOOPED DOWN OVER the National Tennis Center in Queens, New York, and headed toward nearby LaGuardia Airport. On the court below nineteen-year-old Steffi Graf, of Germany, seemed not to notice the jet's noise. Her thoughts were only of winning the 1988 U.S. Open.

Earlier in the year she had won the championships in Australia, France, and England. Now she was just one match point away from adding the American title to this collection. If she succeeded she would become only the third woman ever to accomplish a Grand Slam.

Across the net from Steffi Graf, eighteen-year-old Gabriela Sabatini, of Argentina, crouched behind the baseline. The ball came to her low and spinning off the hard surface. She rushed to meet it, hitting a deep forehand drive.

With long graceful strides Graf raced to return the shot. Her racquet sliced through the muggy air like a knife. Whap! The ball rocketed from the strings to a far corner.

Sabatini responded with a crosscourt return. Graf sprinted to the net, chopping the ball into the opposite forecourt. Again Sabatini fought off defeat, angling a soft slice along the sideline.

Moving to her backhand, Graf slashed a winner that nearly tore the racquet from Sabatini's hand.[1] The contest was over—point, game, and match. In honor of her Grand Slam victories, Graf received a bracelet with four diamonds from the United States Tennis Association.[2]

Tall and lean, Steffi Graf hits the ball as hard as some men. Her forehand is particularly powerful. Special timers have clocked her serve at more than 100 miles an hour. What's more,

Graf's footwork on the court is second to none. "I always take the risk," she said, "no matter what stage of the match."[3]

The people who know Graf say she loves tennis simply for the sake of the game. In practice she never gives less than her best effort. She hits each shot as though it was going to decide a tournament match. And with every swing of her racquet she tries for a winner. Unlike Chris Evert, she is not content to stay on the baseline and force her opponent to make errors. She wants to take command of the situation, to force the action.

When Graf arrived on the women's professional tour it wasn't long before she earned the respect of the other players. She had unusually quick reflexes which enabled her to reach even the most difficult returns. But it was a relentless, attacking style that really set her apart from the field. At every opportunity she would go to the net and use her natural power to overwhelm the opposition. Today, she is very nearly in a class by herself.

Graf best displayed her speed, strength, and daring while winning the 1993 Virginia Slims Championships. In the finals she used her big serve and blazing forehand. She beat Spain's Arantxa Sanchez Vicario—the second ranked woman player in the world—6–1, 6–4, 3–6, 6–1. Afterward Steffi said, "It's been a great, great year, and this is the way you want to end it."[4]

In addition to her 1988 Grand Slam title, Steffi Graf won the gold medal at the Olympic Games in Seoul, Korea.

After season-ending knee surgery in 1997, Graf returned to the tour in 1998, reaching 103 career tournament victories by the year's end. Steffi Graf retired from competitive tennis in 1999.

STEFFI GRAF

BORN: June 14, 1969, Bruhl, Germany.

HEIGHT: 5 feet, 9 inches; WEIGHT: 132 pounds

EDUCATION: Local elementary, secondary schools. No college.

HONORS: One-hundred-three singles titles; More than six hundred singles matches; Member German Federation Cup Team: 1986, 1987, 1989–1992; Ranked No. 1 Women Player in the World: 1987–1990, 1993–1996.

CAREER EARNINGS: $21,839,777.

Practicing is fun for steffi Graf. She especially enjoys reaching and returning a good shot. If every ball is hit to the best of her ability, she knows that winning will take care of itself.

BILLIE JEAN KING

MARIA BUENO MOVED WITH AN effortless grace. Her forehand smash cut crosscourt on a line. Just as the ball cleared the net, Billie Jean King came rushing forward to meet it. The result was a sharply hit drop shot that brought the third and deciding set to match point. A tidal wave of applause flowed through the crowded stands at the All England Tennis Club.

On the next exchange, King scored again with an off-balance volley. Then a perfectly placed lob followed by another volley and a backhand bullet to the opposite corner won her the 1966 Wimbledon title. It was her first victory in this most prestigious of tournaments after six long years of trying.

With a squeal of delight she tossed her racquet high into the air.[1] Suddenly, at twenty-two, the "little girl who plays the man's game" sat atop the world of tennis.[2]

After the trophy presentation reporters asked what changes she had made in her game to become a winner. "I've stopped chattering [talking on court] and started concentrating," she said.[3]

King believed in being aggressive, in going to the net at every opportunity. She was widely regarded as the best serve-and-volley player in women's tennis.

In 1967 she used an overpowering mix of shots to defeat Ann Haydon Jones, 11–9 and 6–4, for the U.S. Open title.

Billie Jean King won all the major tournaments tennis has to offer. But she was at her best when performing on Wimbledon's famed Centre Court. With twenty Wimbledon titles, Billie Jean King holds the record for most titles won at the All-England Championship.

BILLIE JEAN KING

Billie Jean King's attacking game and outspoken manner made headlines and drew spectators into stadiums the world over. She knew that women's tennis needed colorful personalities as well as exciting play to be successful.

In 1975 Billie Jean King needed only forty minutes to defeat Evonne Goologong Cawley, 6–0 and 6–1, in the Wimbledon finals. That day she gave perhaps her best performance ever, completely dominating play at the net. "It's as close as I've come to a perfect match," she said afterward.[4]

King was just as forceful when fighting for equal treatment of women in professional tennis. In 1973 she started the Women's Tennis Association. The following year she founded the Women's Sports Foundation and World Team Tennis. And today she still is outspoken against inequality toward women both on and off the court.

There is much Billie Jean King can look back on with pride. Besides winning 71 professional tournaments she was the first woman athlete to earn more than $100,000 in a single season. For a record twelve years she shared the No. 1 ranking on the United States doubles list. She also was the top rated woman tennis player in the world five times between 1966 and 1972. Her accomplishments in Grand Slam events are second to none.

But she is not a person to think in the past. Though her name no longer makes headlines she remains a leading promoter of tennis at all levels. In 1993, she directed World Team Tennis (WTT) to new heights on two fronts. The professional division played before more than 200,000 fans throughout the country. Meanwhile, the WTT's Recreational League was sponsoring a series of nationwide clinics which introduced some 70,000 young people to tennis as the sport of a lifetime.

Ann Haydon Jones once said, "I found Billie Jean hard to play because her personality was so strong. She never got down on herself. And she never quit. Her mannerisms gave you the impression that she was in control. Every great champion possesses that same confident presence."[5]

BORN: November 22, 1943, Long Beach, California.

HEIGHT: 5 feet, 4-1/2 inches; WEIGHT: 134 pounds.

EDUCATION: Local public elementary, high schools, Los Angeles State University.

HONORS: Member U.S. Federation Cup Team, 1963-1967, 1976-1979; U.S. Wightman Cup Team, 1961-1967, 1970, 1977, 1978; Ranked No. 1 Woman Player in the World: 1966-1968, 1971, 1972, Founded Women's Tennis Association: 1973, Founded Women's Sports Foundation: 1974; Founded World Team Tennis: 1974; International Tennis Hall of Fame, 1987.

CAREER EARNINGS: $1,966,487.

Energy and imagination marked Billie Jean King's career on court. Now she uses these to promote tennis for people of all ages and particularly to help young women with talent to be top professionals.

MARTINA NAVRATILOVA

IT WAS JULY 7, 1990. The women's finals of the All England Championships were under way. Martina Navratilova had never wanted to win so badly. Now only a few points and Zina Garrison-Jackson stood between her and a special place in tennis history.

With a sweeping overhand motion Navratilova slammed a serve crosscourt into the corner of the service box. Garrison-Jackson lunged to make the return. But Garrison-Jackson's shot failed to clear the net.

"Advantage, Ms. Navratilova."

Reaching high, Navratilova leaned into another big serve. The ball skidded low off the closely clipped grass. Once more Garrison-Jackson's shot hit the net, failing to go over it.

"Advantage, Ms. Navratilova." It was now match point.

The ball and Navratilova's racquet met again. This time Garrison-Jackson answered with a forehand smash. Navratilova came forward quickly, sending a soft slice down the sideline. Then Garrison-Jackson slashed a hard backhand on the run. Navratilova turned and watched as the ball bounced long.[1] The match was over.

Cheering exploded through the stands surrounding Wimbledon's famous Centre Court. Navratilova threw back her head and thrust both arms to the sky.[2] At thirty-three, she had won the prestigious tournament for a record ninth time!

"I knew I had one more [title] in me," she said, tears filling her eyes.[3]

Reporters asked if she planned to retire after breaking a mark that had stood for so many years. "I always said I'd play

MARTINA NAVRATILOVA

Early in her career, Martina Navratilova was said to be one of those players who never won the big tournaments. But she proved her critics wrong, winning all the major titles that tennis has to offer.

until I'm thirty, and then I'd see," she told them. "Well, I'm still seeing."[4]

Navratilova left her native Czechoslovakia for the United States in 1975. At first she enjoyed American culture and food. Then she began training with weights and doing a variety of conditioning exercises every day. Soon she became the fittest player in women's tennis. As a result she topped the world rankings in 1978, 1979, and from 1982 to 1986.

In 1993, Navratilova turned thirty-six and was slowed by sore knees. But she still had the strength and stamina to beat the best. She met Monica Seles, then ranked No. 1, in the finals of the Open Gaz de France in Paris. They each won a set and then played to a tiebreaker in the third.

With the score 3–3 in the tiebreak set, Martina took charge. A bullet-like volley, a service ace, and a pair of blistering passing shots gave her a four-point sweep and the match. She simply overpowered the teenaged Seles. "I will look back at this one with undiluted pleasure," Martina said afterward.[5]

Early in 1994 Navratilova announced that she would retire from singles competition at the end of the season. She no longer could perform to the best of her ability. Balls that she once returned easily were now just beyond her reach. She still had the heart of a champion. Her skills were as sharp as ever. And she wanted to win just as badly. But the physical stress of the game she began playing competitively at age eight had taken its toll. In the years ahead she need have no regrets. There was simply nothing left for her to prove.

She has won 166 tournaments, including 18 Grand Slam championships, nearly 1,400 singles matches, and $19,432,645 in prize money! Many experts rate Martina Navratilova as the greatest woman tennis player of all time. And they just might be right.

MARTINA NAVRATILOVA

BORN: October 18, 1956, Prague, Czechoslovakia (now a U.S. citizen).

HEIGHT: 5 feet, 8 inches; WEIGHT: 145 pounds.

EDUCATION: Elementary, secondary schools in Revnice, Czechoslovakia. No college.

HONORS: One Hundred Sixty-six singles titles (record); Nearly
fourteen hundred singles matches (record); Member U.S.
Federation Cup Team: 1982–1986, 1989; Member U.S.
Wightman Cup Team: 1983; Member Czechoslovakian
Federation Cup Team: 1975; Ranked No. 1 Woman Player
in the World: 1978, 1979, 1982–1986.

CAREER EARNINGS: $19,432,645.

Martina Navratilova is one of the few left-handed players in tennis to
attain superstar status. Maureen Connolly was naturally left-handed
but became a great champion playing right-handed.

GABRIELA SABATINI

GABRIELA SABATINI WAS TIRED. If she hoped to win, it would have to be now.[1] The scoreboard at the United States Tennis Association (USTA) Tennis Center in New York told the story. She had won the first set, 6–2. It was 4–4 in the eleven-point tiebreaker that would decide the second set. The hot sun reflected brightly off the hard surface as she started to serve.

With a graceful sweeping motion Steffi Graf drove a bullet-like forehand to the opposite court. The ball came in spinning and kicked low. Sabatini sliced a return down the near sideline. Crossing quickly, Graf attempted a half volley. But she missed and dumped the ball into the net.

"Advantage, Ms. Sabatini," announced the referee.

Graf returned the next serve with another forehand smash. The shot looked to be a winner until Sabatini spun half around and backhanded the ball into a far corner. The crowd roared. Gabriela Sabatini led, 6–4. Victory was just one point away.

Desperate now, Graf rushed the net. But she was driven back with a perfectly placed lob. Graf returned the lob from behind the baseline. Then Gabriela Sabatini chop-volleyed the ball into the forecourt. Lunging, Graf hit the ball long. Sabatini had won the tiebreaker, 7–4, and the 1990 U.S. Open title.

Sabatini thrust her arms into the air with a shout.[2] She had finally captured a major championship. The New York crowd roared its approval. "I can't believe I won the tournament," she told reporters. "It's the greatest feeling. I have no words to express this emotion."[3]

GABRIELA SABATINI

When Gabriela Sabatini finally decides to call it quits as a tennis player, she will step right into a thriving cosmetics business. There are already several fragrances that bear her name.

Unlike other championship matches she had played, Gabriela Sabatini took more chances this time. She frequently changed tactics and wasn't afraid to play at the net. But it was her never-say-die attitude that made the difference. Graf said, "Gabriela is always a good fighter and she really stayed in there against me today. She deserved to win."[4]

The two women met again in the final of the 1991 All England Championships at Wimbledon. After they split the first two sets, Sabatini started to slow down on the fast grass of Centre Court. Her blistering returns began losing their punch, which allowed Graf to increase the pace.

With the score tied at 4–4, Gabriela Sabatini went on the offensive. But her serves lacked their usual low hard line. She could only "sail wounded duck after wounded duck across the net and watch them all fly back in her face."[5] As a result, Steffi Graf hung on to win Wimbledon's coveted trophy.

"It was just another battle with Steffi," Sabatini said later. "She returned very well and I had a little bit of bad luck there at the end. That's how it goes sometimes."[6]

After that Gabriela Sabatini concentrated on improving her endurance and strength. She served much harder and her groundstrokes were among the most powerful in women's professional tennis.

Sabatini's retirement from tennis in 1996 took many by surprise. Her final tournament ended in a first-round loss. Motivation problems and injuries contributed to her decision to retire, but she will always be remembered for her impact on the tennis world.

GABRIELA SABATINI

BORN: May 16, 1970, Buenos Aires, Argentina.

HEIGHT: 5 feet, 8 inches; WEIGHT: 130 pounds.

EDUCATION: Private elementary, secondary schools. No college.

HONORS: Twenty-five singles titles; Member Argentinian Federation Cup Team: 1985-1987; Argentinian Olympic Team: 1988.

CAREER EARNINGS: $8,785,850.

Although quiet and unassuming off the court, Gabriela Sabatini presents a much different image when playing a match. She puts all of her emotion into every shot and never quits until the last point is scored.

MONICA SELES

On March 11, 1991, Monica Seles became the youngest women ever to be ranked No. 1 in the world. She was only seventeen years old at the time. She is also an accomplished ice skater.

Tall And Lean, Monica Seles covered the Madison Square Garden court with long strides. After more than three hours of running on the hard artificial surface she still seemed fresh and eager. Now, in the midst of a record-setting fifth set, she continued to attack on every shot.

A forehand smash drove Gabriela Sabatini deep to the baseline. The return arched high above the net. Monica Seles rushed forward, hitting a drop volley to the opposite side. Point! The capacity crowd cheered and whistled with typical New York enthusiasm.

"Sheer power, determination, and bullet-like finesse" marked Seles' every move.[1] The ball rocketed off the strings of her racquet and kicked low into the corners. Across the net Gabriela Sabatini desperately stretched for the ball. She reached it to stay in the match. But clearly time was running out on her.

In a go-for-broke effort Sabatini began swinging all out on every shot. As she later explained, "I decided to start attacking. It was the only way I could beat her."[2] But Seles stayed calm and kept hitting the ball hard and deep.

The spectators loved the exciting exchanges and loudly voiced their approval. Finally, Seles slammed a crosscourt backhand that ended the contest. The 1990 Virginia Slims Championship was hers—6–4, 5–7, 3–6, 6–4, 6–2. At sixteen, she became the youngest player ever to win the tournament. "It was an unbelievable match," she said afterward. "We both played great. Women's tennis is at its best right now."[3]

Although slight of build, she gets extra power into her shots with a two-handed swing on both her forehand and backhand shots. She also tries to reach each ball as soon as possible, catching it on the rise. This strategy allows her to hit lower and deeper returns. Pretty soon the opposition is forced to play faster and run harder.[4]

When Monica Seles turned pro in 1988 she was only fourteen years old. But she quickly made a name for herself. In 1991 she replaced Steffi Graf as the No. 1 ranked woman player in the world. Monica Seles and Steffi Graf have fought some classic tennis battles since then. One of them took place in the finals of the 1993 Australian Open.

It was a match of power against power. Each player won a set. Then Monica Seles stepped up the pace of the play. Despite the heat she rushed to meet each return. And her serve was clocked at more than 100 miles per hour.

Steffi Graf tried to slow down the pace of play with well-timed lobs. But Seles would not be denied. She went to match-point advantage with a baseline winner. Moments later a forced error by Graf gave Seles the victory. At nineteen, she had won her third straight Australian Open title. "I think this is the most satisfying of the three," Seles said. "I never thought I'd do so well in Grand Slam events."[5]

In early 1993 Seles was playing in Hamburg, Germany when a spectator stabbed her in the back with a knife. Fortunately, the wound was not fatal. Still, it kept her from competing for the rest of the season. At the time of the attack she led the women's professional tennis rankings.

Several months later she went back into training. When Monica Seles returned in 1995 she was co-ranked no. 1. She continued to win titles as her strength returned. Seles became the first woman in the Open Era to win the Canadian Open three consecutive years when she won the title in 1997. She ended the 1997 season ranked fifth and contines her fight for the top in 2000. She won a bronze medal at the 2000 Olympics in Sydney, Australia.

Monica Seles

BORN: December 2, 1973, Novi Sad, Yugoslavia.

HEIGHT: 5 feet, 9-1/2 inches; WEIGHT: 130 pounds.

EDUCATION: Private elementary, secondary schools. No college.

HONORS: Thirty-two singles titles; International Tennis Federation Women's World Champion: 1991, 1992; Tennis Magazine Female Rookie of the Year: 1989; Ranked No. 1 Woman Player in the World: 1991, 1992, 1995 (Co-ranked).

CAREER EARNINGS: $10,615,374.

One day Monica Seles would like to become a professional model. Already she has appeared on the covers of *Vogue, Elle,* and *Seventeen* magazines. She also plans to attend college and study acting.

NOTES BY CHAPTER

Maureen Connolly

1. Allison Danzig, "Miss Connolly Turns Back Miss Fry in Final of National Tennis," *The New York Times*, Sec. C (September 6, 1951), p. 41.
2. Allison Danzig, "Miss Connolly Wimbledon Victor," *The New York Times*, Sec. CI (July 6, 1952), p. V1.
3. Ibid., p. V5.
4. Billie Jean King with Cynthia Starr, *We Have Come a Long Way—The Story of Women's Tennis* (New York: McGraw-Hill Book Company/Regina Ryan Publishing Enterprises, Inc. 1988), p. 81.

Margaret Court

1. Fred Tupper, "Mrs. Court Sets Back Mrs. King, 14–12, 11–9, in 2-1/2 Hour Final at Wimbledon," *The New York Times*, Vol. CXIX (July 4, 1970), p. 15.
2. Ibid.
3. Ibid.
4. *The Lincoln Library of Sports Champions*, (Columbus, OH: The Frontier Press Company, 1989), Vol. 6, p. 124.
5. Ibid., p. 126.
6. Ibid., p. 129.

Chris Evert

1. Fred Tupper, "Chris Evert Captures the Wimbledon Title," *The New York Times*, Vol. CXXIV (July 6, 1974), p. A11.
2. From New Dispatches, "Evert on Top," *The Washington Post*, No. 213 (July 6, 1974), p. C6.
3. Steve Cady, "Chris: 'Never Thought I'd Win'," *The New York Times*, Vol. CXXIV (September 7, 1975), p. V1.
4. *United States Tennis Association Official Encyclopedia of Tennis* (New York: Harper & Row Publishers, 1979), Vol. 8, p. 404.
5. Larry Lorimer, *The Tennis Book*, 5th ed. (New York: Random House, Inc., 1980), p. 59.
6. John Feinstein, "Evert Wins French Open for 7th Time," *The Washington Post*, No. 185 (June 8, 1986), p. B14.

Zina Garrison-Jackson

1. *United States Tennis Association Official Encyclopedia of Tennis* (New York: Harper & Row Publishers, 1979), Vol. 8, p. 404.
2. John Feinstein, *Hard Courts* (New York: Villard Books, 1991), p. 335.
3. Malcolm Morgan, "Open 'Villain' Gracious in Victory," *The New York Times*, Vol. CXXXVIII (September 6, 1991), p. D23.
4. Sally Jenkins, "Navratilova Stands Alone Over All England," *The Washington Post*, No. 215 (July 8, 1990), p. D12.
5. Arthur Ashe, "Garrison's Arsenal Needs One Lethal Weapon," *The Washington Post*, No. 215 (July 8, 1990), p. D12.

Althea Gibson

1. Fred Tupper, "Gibson Wimbledon Victor," *The New York Times*, Vol. CVI (July 7, 1957), p. V1.
2. Ibid.
3. Emma Harrison, "Althea, Pride of One West Side, Become Queen of Another," *The New York Times*, Vol. CVI (September 9, 1957), p. L33.
4. Billie Jean King with Cynthia Starr, "We Have Come A Long Way–The Story of Women's Tennis" (New York: McGraw-Hill Book Company/Regina Ryan Publishing Enterprises, Inc., 1988), p. 74.

5. *The Lincoln Library of Sports Champions*, p. 103.

Steffi Graf

1. Peter Alfano, "Open Victory Gives Graf a Grand Slam," *The New York Times*, Vol. CXXXVII (September 11, 1988), Section 8, p. 9.
2. Peter Alfano, "Virtually Unbeatable," *The New York Times*, Vol. CXXXVII (September 11, 1988), Section 8, p. 9.
3. Billie Jean King with Cynthia Starr, "We Have Come A Long Way–The Story of Women's Tennis" (New York: McGraw-Hill Book Company/Regina Ryan Publishing Enterprises Inc., 1988), p. 189.
4. Robin Finn, "Graf at Top of Her Game, If Not in Tiptop Condition," *The New York Times*, Vol. CXLIII (November 22, 1993), p. C2.
5. King with Starr, p. 188.

Billie Jean King

1. Billie Jean King with Cynthia Starr, "We Have Come A Long Way–The Story of Women's Tennis" (New York: McGraw-Hill Book Company/Regina Ryan Publishing Enterprises Inc., 1988), p. 113.
2. Fred Tupper, "Mrs. King Returns Wimbledon Tennis Title to U.S.," *The New York Times*, Vol. CXV (July 3, 1966), p. V9.
3. Ibid., p. V14.
4. King with Starr, p. 117.
5. Fred Tupper, "Mrs. King Wins Her Sixth Wimbledon Singles Title, 6–0, 6–1," *The New York Times*, Vol. CXXIV (July 5, 1975), p. 11.

Martina Navratilova

1. Sally Jenkins, "Navratilova Stands Alone Over All England," *The Washington Post*, No. 215 (July 8, 1990), p. D1.
2. Billie Jean King with Cynthia Starr, "We Have Come A Long Way–The Story of Women's Tennis" (New York: McGraw-Hill Book Company/Regina Ryan Publishing Enterprises Inc., 1988), p. 175.
3. Jenkins, p. D12.
4. Sally Jenkins, "At Peace, Martina," *The Washington Post*, No. 220 (July 13, 1990), p. F6.
5. Associated Press Report, "For a Day, Navratilova Feels Like No. 1," *The New York Times*, Vol. CXLII (February 22, 1993), p. C7.

Gabriela Sabatini

1. Sally Jenkins, "Sabatini Comes of Age, Halts Graf," *The Washington Post*, No. 278 (September 9, 1990), p. C6.
2. Jenkins, p. C1.
3. Ibid.
4. Ibid., p. C6.
5. Michael Mewshaw, *Ladies of the Court—Grace and Disgrace on the Women's Tennis Tour* (New York: Crown Publishers, Inc., 1993), p. 157.
6. Robin Finn, "Graf Reclaims Her Grit and Title," *The New York Times*, Vol. CXL (July 7, 1991), Section 8, p. 7.

Monica Seles

1. Alison Muscatine, "Seles Beats Sabatini in 5-Set Final," *The Washington Post*, No. 349 (November 19, 1990), p. C1.
2. Ibid., p. C4.
3. Ibid.
4. Michael Mewshaw, *Ladies of the Court—Grace and Disgrace on the Women's Tennis Tour* (New York: Crown Publishers, Inc., 1993), p. 33.
5. Christopher Clary, "Another Australian Open, Another Seles Title," *The New York Times*, Vol. CXLII (January 30, 1993), p. L29.

INDEX